5196 73 29

OCT 2 2 2003

D0928092

PROPERTY
OF THE
FARGO PUBLIC LIBRARY

OCT 2 2 2002

SandCastle

Compound Words

key + board =
keyboard

Amanda Rondeau

Consulting Editor Monica Marx, M.A./Reading Specialist

ABDO Publishing Company

Published by SandCastle™, an imprint of ABDO Publishing Company, 4940 Viking Drive, Edina, Minnesota 55435.

Copyright © 2004 by Abdo Consulting Group, Inc. International copyrights reserved in all countries. No part of this book may be reproduced in any form without written permission from the publisher. SandCastle™ is a trademark and logo of ABDO Publishing Company.

Printed in the United States.

Credits
Edited by: Pam Price
Curriculum Coordinator: Nancy Tuminelly
Cover and Interior Design and Production: Mighty Media
Photo Credits: BananaStock Ltd, Brand X Pictures, Corbis Images, Eyewire Images, Hemera, PhotoDisc, Rubberball Productions, Stockbyte

Library of Congress Cataloging-in-Publication Data

Rondeau, Amanda, 1974-
    Key + board = keyboard / Amanda Rondeau.
      p. cm. -- (Compound words)
    Includes index.
    Summary: Illustrations and easy-to-read text introduce compound words related to school.
    ISBN 1-59197-434-8
    1. English language--Compound words--Juvenile literature. [1. English language--Compound words.] I. Title: Key plus board equals keyboard. II. Title.
PE1175 .R666 2003
428.1--dc21
                                                              2003048006

SandCastle™ books are created by a professional team of educators, reading specialists, and content developers around five essential components that include phonemic awareness, phonics, vocabulary, text comprehension, and fluency. All books are written, reviewed, and leveled for guided reading, early intervention reading, and Accelerated Reader® programs and designed for use in shared, guided, and independent reading and writing activities to support a balanced approach to literacy instruction.

Let Us Know

After reading the book, SandCastle would like you to tell us your stories about reading. What is your favorite page? Was there something hard that you needed help with? Share the ups and downs of learning to read. We want to hear from you! To get posted on the ABDO Publishing Company Web site, send us e-mail at:

sandcastle@abdopub.com

SandCastle Level: Transitional

A compound word is two words joined together to make a new word.

key + board =

keyboard

Bonnie thinks computers are fun.

She likes to use the keyboard.

white + board =

whiteboard

Josh writes on the whiteboard in math class.

after + noon =

afternoon

The playground is a
fun place to play in
the afternoon.

note + book =

notebook

Devon is working on language.

He is writing in his notebook.

back + pack =

backpack

Jenna takes her backpack to school every day.

home + work =

homework

Jim and his sister do homework after school.

The Lost Eyeglasses

"I lost my eyeglasses!" Mrs. Lee said when she came in the room.

"Will you help me search the classroom?"

Ann looked under the keyboard
and on the chalkboard tray.

Jan and Deb searched their
backpacks and dug in the clay.

Tony looked under the notebook
and on the overhead.

"Oops!" Mrs. Lee said.

"I found them on my head!"

More Compound Words

blackboard	laptop
breakdown	lunchtime
classmate	meltdown
coatroom	notepad
desktop	schoolbook
hallway	schoolhouse
homeroom	schoolteacher
knapsack	textbook

Glossary

backpack   a large bag that is worn on a person's back

chalkboard   a hard, smooth surface that you write on with chalk

eyeglasses   lenses contained in a frame that help you see better

notebook   a book with blank pages for taking notes

whiteboard   a white, glossy surface that you write on with erasable markers

About SandCastle™

A professional team of educators, reading specialists, and content developers created the SandCastle™ series to support young readers as they develop reading skills and strategies and increase their general knowledge. The SandCastle™ series has four levels that correspond to early literacy development in young children. The levels are provided to help teachers and parents select the appropriate books for young readers.

Emerging Readers
(no flags)

Beginning Readers
(1 flag)

Transitional Readers
(2 flags)

Fluent Readers
(3 flags)

These levels are meant only as a guide. All levels are subject to change.

To see a complete list of SandCastle™ books and other nonfiction titles from ABDO Publishing Company, visit **www.abdopub.com** or contact us at:

4940 Viking Drive, Edina, Minnesota 55435 • 1-800-800-1312 • fax: 1-952-831-1632